The Tabernacle

Leader Guide

Shawn Barnard, MDiv

with Jeanne Whittaker

This Leader Guide accompanies

The Tabernacle 6-Session DVD-Based Study
(ISBN 9781596366374 or 9781596366381)

and

The Tabernacle Participant Guide (ISBN 9781596366404)

ROSE
PUBLISHING
Torrance, California

The Tabernacle Leader Guide

Copyright © 2013 Bristol Works, Inc.

Rose Publishing, Inc.

4733 Torrance Blvd., #259

Torrance, California 90503 U.S.A.

Email: info@rose-publishing.com

www.rose-publishing.com

Register your Rose Publishing books at

www.rose-publishing.com/register.

Cover art by Ted Larson / www.digitalartbytedlarson.com

All Scripture quotations, unless otherwise indicated, are taken from *The Holy Bible, English Standard Version*. Copyright © 2000; 2001 by Crossway Bibles, a division of Good News Publishers. Used by permission. All rights reserved.

Printed in the United States of America

Contents

Experience the Tabernacle

Have you ever considered that God wants to dwell with you and in you? Think about it: The God of the universe, who created all things, desires to dwell *with* you and *in* you. Unfolded in the pages of Scripture is the story of his deep love for us, and the extent to which he has gone to graciously allow us the privilege to dwell with him in his presence now and for eternity.

But the truth is, you can't approach him casually or on your terms. There is only one way that you can dwell with him now and forever. It is in Jesus Christ that we are restored to God. It is at the cross where we find the hope and assurance that we will always dwell with him, now and forever.

In this series, you will gain insight into part of God's story as seen in the tabernacle. Each article of the tent of meeting has a specific purpose, and clearly reveals God's plan for us to dwell with him, and for him to dwell in us. As you journey through this study, you will discover that everything in Scripture—and in particular, the tabernacle—points to and finds its fulfillment in Jesus Christ. The reality of the tabernacle is that it tells the story of God. And the story of God is that he has always desired to be with us, and for us to be with him.

—Shawn Barnard

Meet the Authors

Shawn Barnard

Pastor Shawn Barnard has been introducing the tabernacle to church groups for many years. He graduated from Ouachita Baptist University with a degree in Religion and Communications, and received his Master of Divinity from Southwestern Baptist Theological Seminary in Fort Worth, Texas.

Shawn is the Senior Pastor of Crossgate Church in Hot Springs, Arkansas, and has been in ministry for over twenty years. He has traveled extensively throughout many countries, equipping pastors and preaching the gospel of Jesus Christ. His passionate desire is to make Christ famous in all the earth.

He and his wife, Jennifer, have three children.

Jeanne Whittaker

Jeanne Whittaker has been in ministry at Capo Beach Church in Capistrano Beach, California for the past thirty years. She founded *The Tabernacle Experience* in 2000 and travels the country providing an interactive spiritual journey through a life-sized tabernacle of the wilderness.

She is passionate about creating an atmosphere where the Spirit can draw others closer to the heart of God, revealing Jesus Christ in every aspect of the tabernacle.

Jeanne and her husband, Craig, live in Dana Point, California. They have three grown children and five grandchildren.

About the Complete DVD-Based Kit

The Complete Kit (ISBN 9781596366374) contains everything you need to get started:

- DVD with six 25 to 30-minute sessions.

- PDF files containing promotional posters, fliers, handouts, bulletin inserts, and banners for you to print as needed.

- One printed Leader Guide and a PDF of the Leader Guide for your iPad or tablet.

- One printed Participant Guide with session outlines, discussion and application questions, definitions, and extra information. Buy additional Participant Guides for each person (ISBN 9781596366404).

- One Tabernacle pamphlet, with a full-color tabernacle diagram identifying each part of the tabernacle and the high priest's garments.

- One ready-to-use Tabernacle PowerPoint® presentation, with 100+ slides to expand the scope of your teaching.

Available at www.TabernacleDVD.com
or www.rose-publishing.com
or by calling Rose Publishing at 1-800-532-4278.
Also available wherever good Christian books are sold.

Register your Rose Publishing books at
www.rose-publishing.com/register.

The Tabernacle Schematic

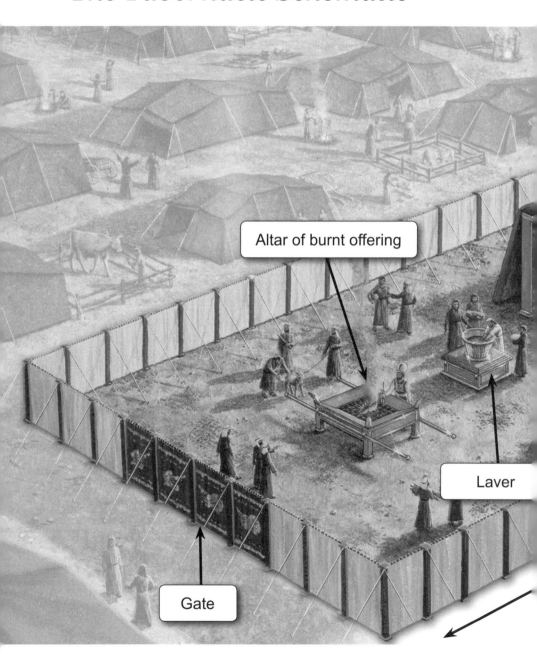

Altar of burnt offering

Laver

Gate

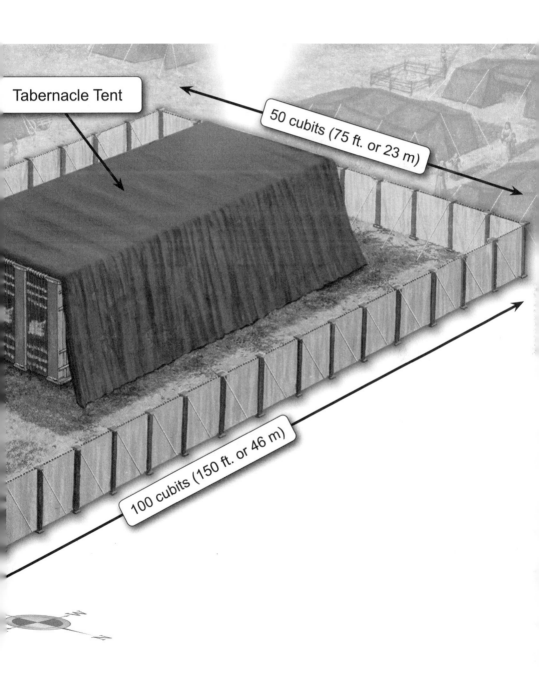

Tabernacle Tent

50 cubits (75 ft. or 23 m)

100 cubits (150 ft. or 46 m)

The Tabernacle Schematic

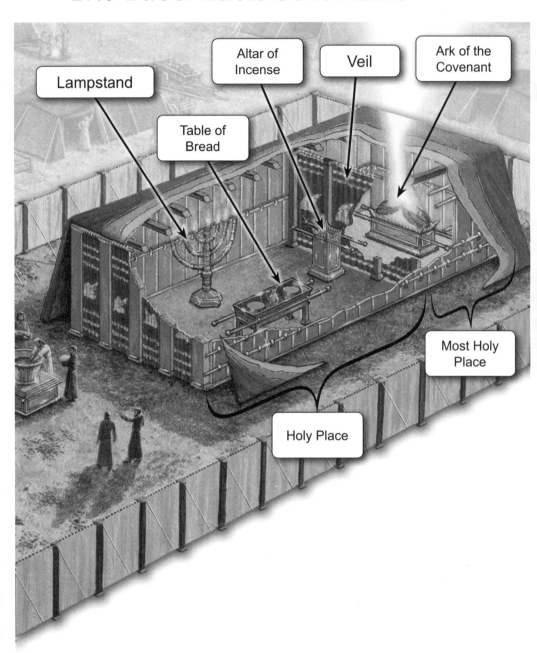

Getting Started

This leader guide has been prepared to equip you to plan and facilitate the DVD-based study of *The Tabernacle*. This study is designed for six 60-minute sessions with the video portion for each session lasting 25 to 30 minutes. The teaching time can be expanded to 90-minute sessions by using *The Tabernacle* PowerPoint® presentation or other study materials included in *The Tabernacle* Complete Kit.

Each class member will need a copy of the participant guide. The participant guide contains:

- Outlines of each video session with "fill in the blanks" that help participants follow along as Pastor Shawn teaches.
- Key Scriptures and "truth statements" for each session.
- Group discussion questions.
- Devotional questions and a Bible study lesson for each session which participants can complete on their own time during the week.
- Glossary and Bible references about the tabernacle.

Participant guides and other tabernacle materials available at www.TabernacleDVD.com or www.rose-publishing.com or by calling Rose Publishing at 1-800-532-4278. Also available wherever good Christian books are sold.

Choosing a Leader

The leader is not a teacher, but rather a facilitator. Years of Bible study and teaching is not required. But the leader, most importantly, must have a desire to explore the Bible, the willingness to be available to others, and be teachable!

The leader will need to coordinate and organize the study and act as an administrator. This will include:

- Promoting the study. Enlist the support of your pastor.

- Announcing the study at church services or in the church bulletin. (See the promotional video on the DVD disc and the PDF promotional materials on the CD.)
- Coordinating enrollment/sign-ups.
- Ordering the Bible study resources.
- If necessary, appointing small group leaders. Conduct a planning session prior to the first class to meet with your small group leaders.

Preparing for Each Session

- Start with prayer. Ask God for guidance as you familiarize yourself with the material in the session, and pray for your group members.
- Watch the DVD session on your own time. (25–30 minutes)
- Complete the lesson in the participant guide for the session.
- For further study, see "More Resources" in this leader guide.
- Make a checklist of all items you will need to bring to the class. For example, DVD, Bible, materials for the group activity, PowerPoint® or other teaching materials you are planning to use.

Format for the Sessions

The class meets weekly to view and follow along with Pastor Shawn's teaching in the video. After watching the video, there is a time for group discussion, which allows participants to benefit from the insights of others. This time provides an arena where participants are free to discuss what they have learned and how they can apply this knowledge to their lives. It will build relationships as group members share with one another and come to the Lord in prayer on one another's behalf. This time also encourages accountability.

Optional:

- Have participants sit around large banquet tables. The tables provide ample room to set out Bibles and participant guides— not to mention coffee! The table creates a sense of security for class members, which helps them to be more vulnerable with the group. Participants are more apt to speak out and share, as the table protects their personal space and acts as a comfort barrier.

- At the end of each chapter in this leader guide you'll find a question and answer on a specific topic related to the session. This can be photocopied or printed and given as a handout to each class member.

Begin Session 1 with welcome, prayer, and introductions. Begin all other sessions promptly with prayer, a quick summary of last week's lesson, and then immediately play the video. (Summaries can be found in this leader guide for each session.)

Optional:

- Encourage participants to arrive 15 minutes prior to the study to engage in fellowship and have some snacks.
- Use peel-and-stick name tags if your class is large and participants may not know each other.
- For introductions, have participants break into pairs. In pairs, take five minutes to introduce yourself to one another. Then, if the class is small (less than 12), have the participants each take one minute to introduce the person they were paired with to the rest of the class. If your class is large, initiate the introduction process in the small group setting. (When individuals do not introduce themselves, but someone else, participants immediately understand how critical it is to be an active listener.)

After watching the video, begin the group discussion time. If your group is large, this is the time to break into smaller groups of 8–12. Decide beforehand how participants will be divided into small groups. Appoint small group leaders before the first class meeting.

There is an optional group activity for each session that can be completed following the group discussion time. Invite members to participate in the activity. Depending on the week, give detailed instructions on how to participate. If the group is large enough to break into smaller groups, participants may engage in the activity at their small group tables.

Always remember, elements of this format may be adjusted according to your preference, schedule, venue, needs, and limitations.

Leading the Group Discussion Time

Like the class leader, small group leaders are not teachers, but facilitators, and need not be versed in the Scriptures; but they must have the willingness to learn and to take the study of the tabernacle seriously. Their main responsibility during the group discussion time is guiding participants to engage with one another and encouraging them to apply what they are learning to their lives.

As you facilitate the group discussion, remember to:

· Emphasize that no one is required to share, but they are encouraged to do so.

· Be flexible, but do not allow the discussion to veer off on a tangent. It's your responsibility to stay on track.

· Allow the Holy Spirit the freedom to direct each session and be sensitive to the signs of God's work as participants share.

Optional:

· You can begin the discussion time with the Old Testament Scripture provided in this leader guide; then close the time with the New Testament Scripture. You can read aloud the verses yourself or have one or two group members read them. (These Scripture verses are also in the participant guides.)

· Wrap up by encouraging participants to complete their homework for the next session—the "Getting into the Word" section—in their participant guides before the next class meeting. Also encourage them to complete their Bible study lesson for this session: the "Further Investigation" and "Personal Reflection" sections in their participant guides.

As a leader, try to create a relaxed atmosphere by communicating acceptance, concern, and encouragement.

- Use first names.
- Don't rush the discussion.
- Briefly comment when participants share: "Thank you for sharing" or "great insight."
- Be sure not to talk too much during the discussion. Periods of silence are okay. Listen intently and be enthusiastic!
- Don't feel threatened or inadequate if someone expects you to be an authority on the Bible or if you don't have all the answers to their questions. Emphasize that your role is to be a facilitator, not a teacher. Participants can learn from one another and, most importantly, from Scripture.
- Should there be a disagreement with the content of the study or a particular view, remember that Scripture is our authority. It's advantageous to the entire group to have a volunteer later delve into Scripture and research the question for the group.
- Don't allow a participant to judge, criticize, or challenge others in a hostile way. If this happens, you may have to address the individual privately.

If you have a class member who dominates the group:

- Situate yourself so as to not make eye contact with this person. (Often participants will read eye contact as a signal to share or to continue sharing.)
- Call on another member of the group and ask if they have something to share.
- Say, "Maybe someone else would like to share."
- Always direct the sharing back to the lesson at hand.

Always remember:

- Participants have signed up for this study to do just that—participate.

- The primary emphasis is to remain on the Bible study.
- Class members will appreciate organization, and starting and ending on time.
- They will also appreciate your commitment to the study and to them. They will look to you as an example of a person who walks in faith, loves God's Word, and possesses a willingness to serve.

Be blessed as you follow God's lead!

More Resources

The Exodus Case by Dr. Lennart Moller (Scandinavia Publishing House; 3rd Extended Edition, 2008)

Messiah in the Feasts of Israel by Sam Nadler (Word of Messiah Ministries, 2006, 2010)

Praying Thru the Tabernacle: A Biblical Model for Effective Prayer by John Courson (Searchlight, 2006)

Rose Guide to the Tabernacle book (Rose Publishing, 2008)

The Tabernacle: Shadows of the Messiah by David M. Levy (The Friends of Israel Gospel Ministry, Inc., 1993)

The Tabernacle Experience www.tabernacleexperience.com (a touring life-size tabernacle of the wilderness)

Dwell: *The Tabernacle*

Dwell: The Tabernacle

Truth Statement

Everything in Scripture points to and finds its fulfillment in Jesus Christ.

Key Verse

> *"And beginning with Moses and all the Prophets, [Jesus] interpreted to them in all the Scriptures the things concerning himself."—Luke 24:27*

Background to the Tabernacle

The children of Israel, God's chosen people, had suffered for years as slaves under the oppressive rule of Pharaoh. It was during this time that God chose Moses to lead them out of the land of Egypt and into the land God had promised them. Where once they were not a people, God was setting apart for himself a treasured people, a kingdom of priests, and a holy nation through whom he would make his glory known.

After leaving Egypt and seeing God display his might in parting the Red Sea, Moses led the Israelites to encamp at the base of Mount Sinai. It was on this mountain that God met with Moses, giving him the Ten Commandments and instructions on how to construct a sanctuary. This sanctuary was called the tabernacle. Because of God's desire to dwell with the children of Israel, and to go before them as they journeyed to the Promised Land, the tabernacle was to be a portable tent where God's presence would dwell among his people (Exodus 20:24–25:9).

As the tabernacle was constructed, God gave Moses detailed instructions of how the tribes were to be arranged around the tent of meeting, as well as specific requirements regarding the materials and the articles of the tabernacle. At all times, the tent of meeting would be at the center of where the twelve tribes of Israel would encamp. Each tribe would face toward the tabernacle, reminding them that they were to keep their focus on God, their King.

God gave the priests, who served as guardians and caretakers of the tabernacle, precise instructions on how to offer acceptable worship to him, provide atonement for the people, and conduct cleansing and purification ceremonies for themselves and the people of Israel. The high priest, who would go into the Most Holy Place (Holy of Holies) once a year, had to follow God's requirements fully—as he, in reverent fear, pulled back the veil and entered into the place where the ark of the covenant rested. It was in the Most Holy Place that God's glory—his very presence—dwelt as a cloud by day and a pillar of fire by night.

The tabernacle, however, was only a foreshadowing of what was to come: the building of the temple by Solomon, the incarnation of Christ, the indwelling presence of God in the lives of all true followers of Jesus Christ, and our future home with him in heaven.

What Participants Will Learn from This Session

- The reality of the tabernacle tells the story of God.
- God's desire is to dwell with us, and for us to be with him.
- We serve a God who is strategic, detailed, and artistic. He is the Master Architect of the heavens and the earth, the tabernacle, and our lives.
- Every article in the tabernacle points to and finds its fulfillment in Jesus.

Opening the Session (15 minutes)

- Open the class time by leading the group in prayer.
- Introduce yourself to the group—not only who you are, but also why you've chosen the tabernacle as the topic of study.
- Do participant introductions as a class or in the small groups.
- Note that there is no "Getting into the Word" section for Session 1; participants can read the "Background to the Tabernacle" section in their participant guides. This will help them have a basic understanding of what the tabernacle was.

Viewer Guide (30 minutes)

The viewer guide helps participants follow along with Pastor Shawn's teaching as they watch the video. (The answers are blank in the participant guide, but are filled in here.)

Session 1
Dwell: The Tabernacle

1. Everything in Scripture _____*points*_____ to and finds its _____*fulfillment*_____ in Jesus Christ.

2. The Tabernacle (Exodus 25:1–9)

   a. The word "sanctuary" means a _____*sacred/holy*_____ place.

   b. God should not be treated as _____*common*_____.

   c. God chooses the insignificant to fill with his _*significance*_.

   d. The tabernacle had only _*one*_ entrance; There is only _*one*_ way to the presence of God—our High Priest, Jesus Christ (John 14:6).

   e. The Levites were the _____*caretakers*_____, _*guardians*_ and _____*mediators*_____ of the tabernacle.

3. Tribes on the east side:

   a. The _*Messiah*_ came from the tribe of Judah.

   b. The tribe of Issachar carried the weight, the _*work*_, and the _____*burden*_____ —as would Jesus.

   c. Like Jesus, the tribe of Zebulun was a _*haven/refuge*_ for the people.

4. The tabernacle shows the immeasurable ___*worth*___ of Jesus Christ.

5. God is saying:

    a. I will ___*dwell*___ in your midst.

    b. I will ___*meet*___ with you.

    c. I will ___*offer*___ restoration, forgiveness, and life to you.

6. Five takeaways:

    a. God's ___*worth*___ is immeasurable.

    b. God's ___*presence*___ is overwhelming.

    c. God's ___*holiness*___ is incomparable.

    d. God's ___*grace*___ is amazing.

    e. God's ___*love*___ is extravagant.

Group Discussion (15 minutes)

Discuss the following questions with your class or small group *after* watching the video. These questions provide interaction in your group setting. You can jot down any notes you might have in the space provided. Group discussions questions are also listed in the participant guides. If you will be doing the optional group activity after the discussion, you may want to shorten the discussion time.

1. What are you hoping to gain from this study on the tabernacle? What questions about the tabernacle would you like to have answered by the end of this study?

    _____

    _____

    _____

    _____

2. Pastor Shawn reflects on this truth: "The tabernacle tells the story of God. And the story of God is that he has always desired to be with us." What's your reaction to the idea that you're an intricate part of God's story? That God desires to be with you? Explain your answer.

    _____

    _____

    _____

    _____

3. Pastor Shawn observes that the "sanctuary" is a sacred/holy place, and that neither it nor God should be treated as common. In what ways are we often guilty of taking God and his holiness for granted?

    _____

    _____

    _____

4. What's your reaction to Pastor Shawn's observation "God chooses the insignificant to fill with his significance"? How should that affect your perspective toward God? Toward yourself?

_____

_____

_____

_____

5. Think again about the "five takeaways" that Shawn concludes the message with:

   - God's worth is immeasurable.
   - God's presence is overwhelming.
   - God's holiness is incomparable.
   - God's grace is amazing.
   - God's love is extravagant.

Looking at all five of these together, what kind of picture of God does this paint? What do they tell us about the character of God and his attitude toward us?

_____

_____

_____

_____

6. What's *your* takeaway this week after watching this session? What do you think God is trying to tell you through that?

_____

_____

_____

_____

Key Scriptures

Old Testament	New Testament
"I will dwell among the people of Israel and will be their God. And they shall know that I am the LORD their God, who brought them out of the land of Egypt that I might dwell among them. I am the LORD their God." —Exodus 29:45–46	"And the Word became flesh and dwelt among us, and we have seen his glory, glory as of the only Son from the Father, full of grace and truth…. For from his fullness we have all received, grace upon grace. For the law was given through Moses; grace and truth came through Jesus Christ." —John 1:14–17

Group Activity (Optional; 5–10 minutes)

After your group discussion, start playing worship music quietly in the background. Then, ask your group members to remove their shoes.

Once everyone has gotten their shoes off, read **Exodus 3:4–5** to the group: "When the LORD saw that he turned aside to see, God called to him out of the bush, 'Moses, Moses!' And he said, 'Here I am.' Then he said, 'Do not come near; take your sandals off your feet, for the place on which you are standing is holy ground.'"

Then discuss the following questions together:

- What's your holy ground—in other words, a place where you know you've encountered God in his holiness? What else was going on in your life at that time?
- How were you changed by that encounter?

Close your activity/discussion time in prayer, thanking God for how he has been present in our lives, and for the transformation you we already see as a result. Ask God to continue to transform each one of us, that we may be able to increasingly behold his holiness in us.

Where Is Mount Sinai?

Although the Bible names many places the Israelites passed while in the Sinai Peninsula, we do not know with certainty the location of Mt. Sinai. Based on analysis of the Scriptures, archaeology, and geography, scholars have proposed over a dozen different locations for the mountain. Much hinges on the route the Israelites took from Egypt into the Sinai.

The following are some of the most often quoted locations for Mt. Sinai:

- Traditionally the Israelites are thought to have traveled into the southern part of the peninsula, where the following two mountains, which have been identified as Mt. Sinai, are found:

  1. *Jebel (Mount) Serbal*, where Christians built a monastery in the 4th century, is an early suggestion.

  2. *Jebel Musa*, next to Mount Catherine where Saint Catherine's Monastery was built in the 6th century, has long been the most favored of all candidates.

- Of the northern proposed locations, *Jebel Sin Bisher* in the central west part of the peninsula has drawn some scholarly interest in recent years. Although with very little scholarly interest, *Jebel Helal* has also been proposed as a possible location for Mt. Sinai.

- Also in recent years there has been much publicity surrounding the claim that Mt. Sinai is to be identified with *Jebel el-Lawz* in Saudi Arabia. A team of explorers, who did not have professional archaeological or historical training, claimed this place as the site of Mt. Sinai. However, because of serious problems with the team's use of the Scriptures, various mistakes in their use of archaeological and geographical data and methodology, the scholarly community has raised important objections to the validity of that site.

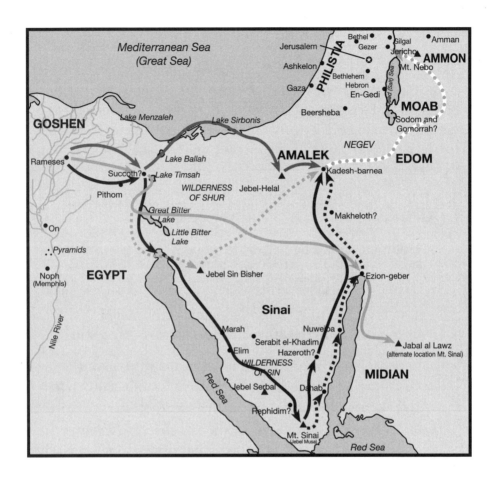

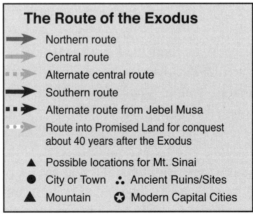

The Route of the Exodus

→ Northern route

→ Central route

▸▸▸ Alternate central route

→ Southern route

▪▪▪▸ Alternate route from Jebel Musa

•••• Route into Promised Land for conquest
about 40 years after the Exodus

▲ Possible locations for Mt. Sinai

● City or Town   ∴ Ancient Ruins/Sites

▲ Mountain   ✪ Modern Capital Cities

Notes:

_____

_____

_____

_____

_____

_____

_____

_____

_____

_____

_____

_____

_____

_____

_____

_____

_____

_____

_____

_____

_____

_____

_____

_____

Notes:

_____

_____

_____

_____

_____

_____

_____

_____

_____

_____

_____

_____

_____

_____

_____

_____

_____

_____

_____

_____

_____

_____

_____

_____

_____

_____

_____

Sacrifice:
The Altar of Burnt Offering

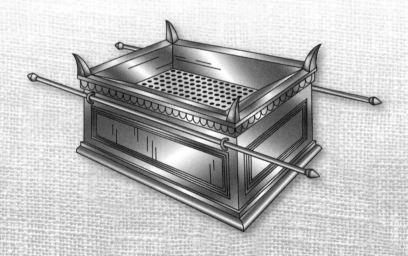

Sacrifice: The Altar of Burnt Offering

Truth Statement

Jesus' sacrifice for us is God's merciful provision, so that we might enter into a relationship with God that is both personal and eternal.

Key Verse

> *"For you will not delight in sacrifice, or I would give it; you will not be pleased with a burnt offering. The sacrifices of God are a broken spirit; a broken and contrite heart, O God, you will not despise."—Psalm 51:16–17*

Getting into the Word

This section is designed to familiarize participants (and leaders too) with what they will learn in the video segment. It should be completed by participants sometime during the week *before* the class meeting. (The answers are filled in here.)

Read **Exodus 27:1–8** and **38:1–7**.

What was the altar of burnt offering made from?

Acacia wood

What metal was used to overlay the altar?

Bronze

In Scripture, bronze refers to or represents judgment. The pillars that supported the courtyard were made of bronze. However, the bases of the courtyard pillars were fashioned from silver. Silver represents redemption. Don't miss this picture: Although the columns are made of bronze, they are set in silver bases—bases of redemption!

The further we journey into the tabernacle, the more valuable the precious metals become. The five columns at the entrance of the tabernacle proper were made of gold and bronze. The four columns within the Holy Place that stand before the veil are made of gold, silver, and bronze. The articles within the Holy Place and the Most Holy Place—the lampstand, the table of bread, the altar of incense, the ark of the covenant, and the mercy seat—are all made of acacia wood overlaid with pure gold.

What were the measurements of the altar?

3 cubits (4 1/2 ft. or 1.38 m) high, 5 cubits (7 1/2 ft. or 2.3 m) wide, and 5 cubits (7 1/2 ft. or 2.3 m) long

What were placed at all four corners of the altar?

Horns

Horns symbolize God's power over life and over death. The priest would sprinkle the blood of the sacrificial animal upon the horns. The blood that poured from the sacrifice—the life of the body—was caught in the basin underneath.

Read **Numbers 4.** You'll discover the details on how the sacred objects were transported, and by whom. Write down some of your observations below.

God's instructions were very detailed about who was appointed to transport the sacred items of the tabernacle, and how they were to care for those items. There was one person, Eleazar the son of Aaron, appointed to have oversight of the whole tabernacle. These instructions came not from man, but from God, as verse 49 makes clear: " ... the commandment of the Lord through Moses."

_____

_____

_____

_____

_____

_____

What Participants Will Learn from This Session

- The altar of burnt offering is to the Old Testament what the cross is in the New Testament.
- The altar of burnt offering is God's provision for reconciliation.

Opening the Session (5 minutes)

Summarize last week's lesson for the class to refresh their memories about what they learned and to help class members who missed last week to catch up with the rest of the class.

- Last week Pastor Shawn gave us an overview of the tabernacle. We learned how detailed and specific God was as he instructed Moses in the building of the tabernacle.
- We also learned of God's constant and persistent desire to dwell with us. And also how the precious metals used in the tabernacle speak of God's immeasurable worth.
- This week we'll learn about at the first item people would see when they entered the Courtyard of the tabernacle: the altar of burnt offering.

Viewer Guide (25 minutes)

The viewer guide helps participants follow along with Pastor Shawn's teaching as they watch the video.

Session 2
Sacrifice: The Altar of Burnt Offering

1. Why have an altar of burnt offering? (Exodus 27:1–8)

    a. God ___*commanded*___ it.

    b. ___*Sacrifice*___ has to be made for the penalty of sin.

2. Why sacrifice?

    a. Sacrifice is God's ___*merciful*___ provision (Psalm 51:1–2).

    b. God's ___*justice*___ demands that sin be paid for (Jeremiah 31:31–34; Hebrews 9:11–15).

3. Jesus is the spotless ___*Lamb*___ of God.

    a. Jesus was ___*examined*___ by religious officials.

    b. Jesus was found to be without ___*blemish/defect*___.

    c. Jesus' sacrifice is God's ___*merciful*___ provision for us (John 3:16).

    d. Christ ___*tabernacled*___ among us (John 1:1, 14).

    e. Christ is ___*in*___ us (John 14).

    f. We will ___*dwell*___ with God forever (Revelation 21:3).

Group Discussion (30 minutes)

Discuss the following questions with your class or small group *after* watching the video.

1. Pastor Shawn said that the tabernacle and its altar of burnt offering were pointing to something much, much bigger. What was he referring to? What is the significance of this?

    _____

    _____

    _____

    _____

2. In Romans 12:1 Paul says, "I appeal to you therefore, brothers, by the mercies of God, to present your bodies as a living sacrifice, holy and acceptable to God, which is your spiritual worship." How can we offer ourselves as living sacrifices? What would that look like for you, personally?

    _____

    _____

    _____

    _____

3. Remember, a sacrifice is something we hold in great value and offer to another. When has God called you to be a living sacrifice, and you acted on that prompting? What was the result?

    _____

    _____

    _____

    _____

    _____

4. Was there a time when you *didn't* act on God's prompting? What was the result in *that* instance?

_____

_____

_____

5. Jeremiah 33:11 tells us that the Lord is good, that his mercy endures forever, and that we should bring him a sacrifice of praise. How would praising God be a sacrifice? Are there times when praising God *isn't* a sacrifice? Explain.

_____

_____

_____

6. Praise is often spontaneous, but often our circumstances are not conducive to praise. When has your praise truly been an exercise in faith and obedience? What did you learn from that experience?

_____

_____

_____

Key Scriptures

Old Testament	New Testament
"For you will not delight in sacrifice, or I would give it; you will not be pleased with a burnt offering. The sacrifices of God are a broken spirit; a broken and contrite heart, O God, you will not despise." —Psalm 51:16–17	"Since, therefore, we have now been justified by his blood, much more shall we be saved by him from the wrath of God. For if while we were enemies we were reconciled to God by the death of his Son, much more, now that we are reconciled, shall we be saved by his life. More than that, we also rejoice in God through our Lord Jesus Christ, through whom we have now received reconciliation." —Romans 5:9–11

Group Activity (Optional; 5–10 minutes)

Before your meeting time: Set up a makeshift cross in the corner of your room (two branches or two pieces of lumber secured together will do). You'll also need a small piece of paper, pen, and a nail for each member of your group, as well as one or more hammers, depending on the size of your group and the size of your cross. (Pushpins are an acceptable substitute for hammer and nails, but less effective.)

At the end of your discussion time, cue the worship music. Distribute a paper and pen to each participant, and ask them to write down their offering to the Lord—be it one of thanks, forgiveness, or something they choose to surrender for Christ's sake (time, activity, etc.). Allow 2–3 minutes for everyone to write.

When everyone is done writing, direct your group members to the cross. Instruct participants to be in an attitude of worship and prayer as they approach the cross and nail their individual offerings to it. (If participants don't want other group members to see what they wrote, tell them to flip their papers over or fold their papers, and assure them that all papers will be destroyed later on, without your looking.)

Close your activity in prayer, thanking God for all he has done in each group member's life and asking God's help in living a life of submission to him.

Why a Blood Sacrifice?

One of the greatest problems for people today with the idea of sacrifice is its inevitable bloodiness. Sacrifice today simply appears primitive and cruel. A brief word about how Old Testament people understood the concept of blood will be helpful for understanding the concept and practice of sacrifice.

The first encounter with blood occurred when Cain struck his brother Abel dead. God voiced the seriousness of Cain's offense: "What have you done? Listen! Your brother's blood cries out to me from the ground" (Genesis 4:10).

In Genesis 9:3–6, God prohibited eating or drinking the blood of animals. The explanation for this prohibition is in Leviticus 17: "For the life of a creature is in the blood, and I have given it to you to make atonement for yourselves on the altar; it is the blood that makes atonement for one's life" (verse 11). The blood of animals had a purpose: atonement.

The question remains: why sacrifice animals? First, remember the apostle Paul's words regarding sin: "For the wages of sin is death" (Romans 6:23). Second, keep in mind that the regulations for sacrifices occur in the context of the tabernacle in the book of Leviticus. Animals became substitutes for humans: a life, an innocent life, for another's life, the life of a guilty one. Animal sacrifice, then, was God's gracious provision for humans. The shedding and use of the animal's blood for the purifying or atoning rituals was a reminder for the worshiper that a life had been taken: the cost of sin is high indeed. The sacrifice of an animal allowed the Israelites to dwell alongside God himself as his presence dwelt in the tabernacle.

Notes:

_____

_____

_____

_____

_____

_____

_____

_____

_____

_____

_____

_____

_____

_____

_____

_____

_____

_____

_____

_____

_____

_____

_____

_____

_____

_____

Notes:

_____

_____

_____

_____

_____

_____

_____

_____

_____

_____

_____

_____

_____

_____

_____

_____

_____

_____

_____

_____

_____

_____

_____

_____

_____

_____

Clean:
The Bronze Laver

Clean: The Bronze Laver

Truth Statement

Through the bronze laver, we are reminded of our own sinfulness and our need to be cleansed by God's Word.

Key Verse

> "Who shall ascend the hill of the LORD? And who shall stand in his holy place? He who has clean hands and a pure heart, who does not lift up his soul to what is false."
> —Psalm 24:3–4

Getting into the Word

This section is designed to familiarize participants (and leaders too) with what they will learn in the video segment. It should be completed by participants sometime during the week *before* the class meeting. (The answers are filled in here.)

Read **Exodus 30:17–21**.

What was the bronze laver used for?

Washing

The priests had to first pass by the altar of burnt offering (the place of forgiveness) before they could participate in the ongoing cleansing at the laver. What parts of their body were they to wash on a continual basis?

Hands and feet

What is the exact location of the laver?

Between the tent of meeting and the altar of burnt offering

Read **Exodus 38:8**. The laver was made of bronze. What particular group of people offered the bronze to fashion the laver? Do you recall where they would have secured these mirrors?

The women who served at the doorway offered the mirrors. They secured the mirrors from the Egyptian women when they left Egypt.

Exodus 29:1–10 describes a washing to consecrate the priests, this was a one-time ritual. This one-time washing is a foreshadowing of how we surrender our lives to God and publicly announce to our community, by the washing of the water at baptism, that we are now set apart for God. Jesus is our example.

Read **John 1:19–34**. Where was Jesus baptized, and by whom?

In the Jordan River by John the Baptist

What Participants Will Learn from This Session

- Through the bronze laver, we see the picture and importance of being cleansed before God.
- God's purity and presence demand continual cleansing.
- We are cleansed by God's Word.

Opening the Session (5 minutes)

Summarize last week's lesson:

Last week Pastor Shawn shared the importance of the altar and sacrifice. The altar in the New Testament is the cross and the sacrifice is the Lamb of God, Jesus Christ. The blood of an innocent, unblemished sacrifice paid for the sin of the guilty.

This week we'll look at the next item in the Courtyard of the tabernacle: the bronze laver.

Viewer Guide (25 minutes)

The viewer guide helps participants follow along with Pastor Shawn's teaching as they watch the video.

Session 3
Clean: The Bronze Laver

(Exodus 30:17–21)

1. The bronze laver was highly _polished_ (Exodus 38:8); thus, the priests would see their own ___*reflection*___ .

2. Why must we be cleansed?

    a. God's ___*purity*___ demands it (1 Peter 1:16).

    b. God's ___*presence*___ demands it (Psalm 24:3–4; Matthew 5:8; Isaiah 6).

3. How are we made clean?

    a. We are covered by Christ's ___*sacrifice*___ (Hebrews 9).

    b. We are cleansed by his ___*righteousness*___ .

    c. As we are cleansed by God's Word, we are ___*transformed*___ by the Word (Ephesians 5:26).

4. What do we need to do?

    a. ___*Gaze*___ into Christ and see that we need to be made clean (Romans 3:23).

    b. ___*Sanctification*___: Letting God's Spirit work in your life to make you more like Jesus.

Group Discussion (30 minutes)

Discuss the following questions with your class or small group *after* watching the video.

1. Because the laver was fashioned from highly polished mirrors, the priests could see their reflection in the water when they washed. What significance do you see here?

    _____

    _____

    _____

2. How does the Word of God cleanse and transform us? What evidence of this can you point to from your own life? Where do you still need cleansing and transformation?

    _____

    _____

    _____

3. Read **John 13:1–15**. What was Jesus teaching his disciples, through his example?

    _____

    _____

    _____

4. How can we participate in the "washing of another's feet"? Give examples.

    _____

    _____

5. What is your takeaway from this session? How will you put it into action?

    _____

    _____

    _____

Key Scriptures

Old Testament	New Testament
"And one called to another and said: 'Holy, holy, holy is the Lord of hosts; the whole earth is full of his glory!' And the foundations of the thresholds shook at the voice of him who called, and the house was filled with smoke. And I [Isaiah] said: 'Woe is me! For I am lost; for I am a man of unclean lips, and I dwell in the midst of a people of unclean lips; for my eyes have seen the King, the Lord of hosts!'"—Isaiah 6:3–5	"If we confess our sins, he is faithful and just to forgive us our sins and to cleanse us from all unrighteousness." —1 John 1:9

Group Activity (Optional; 5–10 minutes)

Before your meeting time: Have one or several large bowls of water, as well as hand towels or paper towels. Place them on a table in the front of your meeting area.

At the end of your discussion time, cue the worship music. Give your group members 2–3 minutes to silently and prayerfully reflect before the Lord and on the sins they need to confess before him. Instruct them to silently confess those sins to him now. After your silent prayer/confession time, have participants "ceremonially" wash their hands, as a sign of their cleansing before the Lord.

You may also want to display the following prayer on a whiteboard or projector screen for group members to silently recite as they wash, or print the prayer on paper for each participant to take home: "Have mercy on me, O God, according to your steadfast love; according to your abundant mercy blot out my transgressions. Wash me thoroughly from my iniquity, and cleanse me from my sin! ... Create in me a clean heart, O God, and renew a right spirit within me" (Psalm 51:1–2, 10).

After everyone has had a chance to wash their hands, close your activity time in prayer, thanking God that "he is faithful and just to forgive us our sins and to cleanse us from all unrighteousness" (1 John 1:9).

Why Were Purity Laws Important in the Old Testament?

The issue of purity was very important for the Israelites. The tabernacle was at the center of all of Israel's life. God's presence in the midst of the camp determined the life of the people. An important function of the Mosaic Law was to instruct people on how to live in the presence of a holy God. The holy and the impure cannot coexist. Thus, God provided a means to cleanse what had become impure. God chose purification rites and sacrifices to prevent the destruction of the people when they became impure. The following table shows the main causes for ritual and moral impurity and the prescription for achieving purity anew.

Jesus changed this situation. The different purification rites and sacrifices in the Old Testament were anticipations of Christ's ministry. Because of the perfect cleansing in Jesus' blood and his perfect sacrifice on the cross, the purification rites and sacrifices are no longer necessary. For this reason, the causes for ritual impurity listed here no longer apply to Christians.

	Ritual Impurity	Moral Impurity
Kind	Unavoidable, since it is part of life. It is not sinful.	Avoidable and directly linked to human sin and disobedience.
Causes	1. Entry of foreign entities into the body (Leviticus 11:39–40). 2. Contact with unclean things (Leviticus 11:24–31). 3. Things exiting the body (Leviticus 13:1–46; 15:1–3). 4. Loss of bodily fluids (Leviticus 12:2; 15:16; 15:25).	1. Idolatry (Leviticus 18:21; 19:31). 2. Certain sexual transgressions (Leviticus 18:6–18; 20:11–14).
Consequences	Impurity is contagious and inevitable. The Israelites had to be aware of their condition and take the necessary steps to avoid contamination. Impurity excluded people from worshiping at the tabernacle, or even remaining in the camp.	Moral impurity is not contagious by touch. However, its effects are broad: They contaminate the individual, the land, and the tabernacle.
Duration	Temporary and short-term.	Temporary but long-lasting.
Undoing	Ritual bathing, offering or sacrifice, waiting.	Atonement, punishment, exile, or even death.

Notes:

_____

_____

_____

_____

_____

_____

_____

_____

_____

_____

_____

_____

_____

_____

_____

_____

_____

_____

_____

_____

_____

_____

_____

_____

_____

_____

_____

Illuminate:
The Lampstand

Illuminate: The Lampstand

Truth Statement

Just as the lampstand was strategically and purposefully placed in the Holy Place, you have been strategically and purposefully placed in the world to shine Christ for his glory.

Key Verse

"Again Jesus spoke to them, saying, 'I am the light of the world. Whoever follows me will not walk in darkness, but will have the light of life.'"—John 8:12

Getting into the Word

This section is designed to familiarize participants (and leaders too) with what they will learn in the video segment. It should be completed by participants sometime during the week *before* the class meeting. (The answers are filled in here.)

Read **Exodus 25:31–40.**

The lampstand was made from what precious metal?

Pure gold

What technique was used to fashion the lampstand?

Hammering

How many branches were on the lampstand?

Six

What was the purpose of the lampstand (see verse 37)?

To give light to the Holy Place

Write out the final statement in Exodus 25 in reference to the lampstand (verse 40).

"And see that you make them after the pattern for them, which is being shown you on the mountain."

Read **Hebrews 1:3.** "Jesus is the radiance of the _glory_ of _God_."

What Participants Will Learn from This Session

- Jesus is the light of the world.
- Light shatters darkness and exposes what is hidden.
- God desires to display his light in us that he will be revealed through us.

Opening the Session (5 minutes)

Summarize last week's lesson:

Last week Pastor Shawn directed us to the bronze laver in the Courtyard. We saw the importance for the priests to clean up after they sacrificed at the altar of burnt offering. Yet they were instructed to clean up even before they began their work, indicating how important it was for them to be continually cleansed before God.

In today's lesson, we will move from the Courtyard into the tabernacle tent–into the Holy Place.

Viewer Guide (25 minutes)

The viewer guide helps participants follow along with Pastor Shawn's teaching as they watch the video.

Session 4
Illuminate: The Lampstand

1. Why a lampstand? (Exodus 25:31–40; 27:20–21)

    a. Light is the essence and expression of God's ___character___ (Genesis 1:1–5; Psalm 27:1).

    b. Light shatters ___darkness___ (John 1:5).

   c. Light exposes what is ___*hidden*___ (1 Corinthians 4:5).

   d. Light gives vision and ___*direction*___ (Psalm 119:105).

   e. Light represents ___*life*___ (John 1:4).

2. Feast of Tabernacles (Leviticus 23:33–44)

   a. Jesus is the living ___*water*___ (John 7:37–38).

   b. Jesus is the ___*light*___ of the ___*world*___ (John 8:12).

3. Jesus is the ___*source*___ of the light of life (Exodus 27:20).

   a. The oil must be ___*pure*___ —speaks of the righteousness of Christ.

   b. The oil must be ___*beaten*___ —Jesus was crushed on our behalf (Isaiah 53:5).

   c. Oil represents ___*healing*___ .

   d. *Olive* means ___*"brightness"*___ and is derived from a phrase that means "mountainside to the east."

4. We have been strategically and purposefully placed in the world to ___*shine*___ Christ for his glory.

Group Discussion (30 minutes)

Discuss the following questions with your class or small group *after* watching the video.

1. The lampstand was beaten from one piece of gold. Remember, all Scripture points to and finds its fulfillment in Christ. How does this technique used to fashion the lampstand relate to Christ?

    _____

    _____

    _____

    _____

    _____

    _____

2. Pastor Shawn related the value of the lampstand to the immeasurable worth of Christ. In your own words, what does it mean that Jesus is of immeasurable worth?

    _____

    _____

    _____

    _____

    _____

    _____

3. Jesus is the light of the world, and calls us to be light *to* the world. How has Jesus given vision and direction in your life? Give a specific example, if you can.

    _____

    _____

    _____

    _____

4. How has Jesus used you to bring light to others? How did you see Christ's glory realized in that?

_____

_____

_____

_____

_____

5. We have been purposefully placed in the world to shine Christ for his glory. How might believing this change your perspective of your position at work? In your family? Your neighborhood? Your marriage? Your church?

_____

_____

_____

_____

_____

_____

Key Scriptures

Old Testament	New Testament
"You shall command the people of Israel that they bring to you pure beaten olive oil for the light, that a lamp may regularly be set up to burn."—Exodus 27:20	"In the same way, let your light shine before others, so that they may see your good works and give glory to your Father who is in heaven." —Matthew 5:16

Group Activity (Optional; 5–10 minutes)

Here are two options for group activities.

Option 1

You will need:

- Seven votive candles and seven glass votive holders (available at most craft stores) arranged in a row.
- Lighters and lighting sticks: wooden skewers work best (available at most grocery markets).
- Scriptures either framed and placed somewhere everyone can see them or printed out and given to each participant:

  "Again Jesus spoke to them, saying, 'I am the light of the world. Whoever follows me will not walk in darkness, but will have the light of life.'"—John 8:12

  "In the same way, let your light shine before others, so that they may see your good works and give glory to your Father who is in heaven."—Matthew 5:16

Place the candles in the glass votive holders. Then place all seven of them in a row. Light each of the candles. The participants will extinguish one of the flames by blowing out the light, then relight the extinguished candle with the lighting stick to show their willingness to allow Christ to shine through them as the light of the world, in their family, friends, neighborhood, workplace, and church. The Scriptures can be posted or printed to recite as the class participates at the "lampstand."

Option 2

Before the session: Figure out how to completely darken your room—not only by locating the light switch, but also by turning the blinds or covering the windows beforehand, if necessary. Also, familiarize yourself with the first set of questions here before you turn off your lights.

After your discussion time, start your worship music, and ask everyone to get up and move to another part of the room, so they're at least 10 feet from where they were sitting (if possible). Then, turn off the lights in your meeting area—and again, make sure you've read the first two questions to yourself before you do it! Then, discuss the following questions:

What do you think would happen if you all tried to find your seats again right now? Why?

When have you felt "in the dark" and unable to find Jesus—either before or since becoming a Christian? Who became light for you during that time?

Turn your lights back on in your meeting area and have everyone sit back in their original seats.

Then discuss: Think about your reaction to the lights coming back on. Why might some people—again, even perhaps Christians—prefer to stay in the darkness? How can we help them get past that?

Notes:

_____

_____

_____

_____

_____

_____

_____

_____

_____

_____

_____

_____

_____

What Is the Hanukkah Menorah?

The word *hanukkah* means "dedication" or "consecration." It refers to the rededication of the temple in Jerusalem. The events celebrated at Hanukkah took place nearly 170 years before Jesus was born. By that time, the portable tabernacle had long since been replaced by a permanent structure—the temple in Jerusalem.

Antiochus "Epiphanes," the King of Syria, defiled the temple in Jerusalem. He placed a statue of the Greek god Zeus in the temple and ordered the Jews to worship it. He also sacrificed a pig inside the temple—the Old Testament considered pigs unclean animals (Leviticus 11:7). This action angered the Jewish people. The priest Mattathias Maccabee and his sons organized fellow Jews and fought a series of battles against Antiochus' army. By a miracle of God the Jews defeated the army of Antiochus and marched into Jerusalem victorious.

Hanukkah is also known as the Feast of Lights or Feast of Dedication in the New Testament because of a legendary miraculous provision of oil for the eternal light in the temple. After cleansing the temple, the supply of oil to relight the eternal flame (the symbol of God's presence) was only enough for one day. But God performed a great miracle, and the flame burned for the additional eight days needed to purify new oil. The flame never went out, and the Jews rededicated the temple. Hanukkah commemorates this event. Therefore, the Hanukkah menorah (candlestick) used in the celebration today has nine candles, one for each day the flame continued to burn. (Note that the lampstand in the tabernacle had seven flames.)

The Gospel of John mentions Jesus celebrating the Feast of Dedication (Hanukkah) at the temple (John 10:22).

Presence: *The Table of Bread and the Altar of Incense*

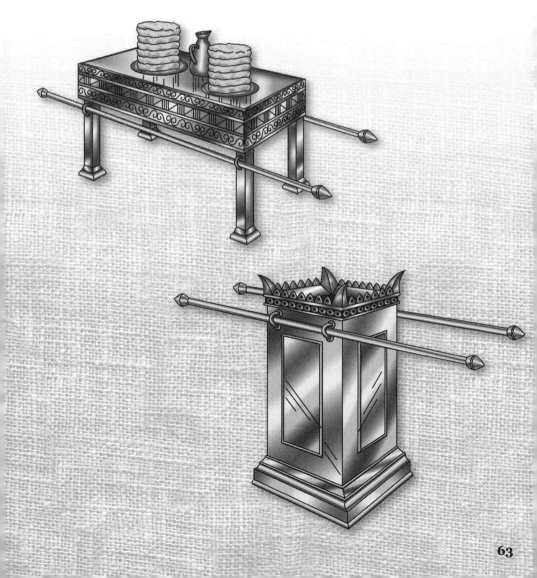

Presence: The Table of Bread and the Altar of Incense

The Table of Bread

Truth Statement

Jesus is our provision. He is our all-in-all. He is our sustenance for life.

Key Verse

"Jesus said to them, 'I am the bread of life; whoever comes to me shall not hunger, and whoever believes in me shall never thirst.'"—John 6:35

The Altar of Incense

Truth Statement

Our prayers, like a sweet aroma, should honor and please God.

Key Verse

"Give ear to my voice when I call to you! Let my prayer be counted as incense before you, and the lifting up of my hands as the evening sacrifice!"—Psalm 141:1–2

Getting into the Word

This section is designed to familiarize participants (and leaders too) with what they will learn in the video segment. It should be completed by participants sometime during the week *before* the class meeting. (The answers are filled in here.)

The Table of Bread

The Hebrew word for bread means both "face" and "presence." The table is near enough to the Most Holy Place to be considered standing in the very presence of God.

Perhaps we can imagine the table being like the manger that held the Bread of Life when he first entered our world—and then later, like the cross on which Jesus hung when he died for our sins. Both of these salvation events occurred before the very face of God.

Read **Exodus 25:23–30; Leviticus 24:5–9**.

What are the measurements of the table?

2 cubits (3 ft. or 92 cm) long, one cubit (1 1/2 ft. or 46 cm) wide, and 1 1/2 cubits (2 1/4 ft. or 69 cm) high

When was the bread set out?

Every Sabbath

Who ate it?

Aaron and his sons (priests)

How many stacks were there, and how many loaves in each stack?

Two stacks; six loaves in each stack

What did the bread represent (see Leviticus 24:8)?

A covenant forever between God and his people

Read **John 6:22–59**. What does Jesus call himself here?

The bread of life

Reread **John 6:27**. Why does Jesus say he will give "the food that endures to eternal life"?

_____Because the Father has set his seal (covenant) on him_____

The Altar of Incense

God gave specific instruction on how the incense was to be made and how it was to be used. God is very detailed, structured, and strategic.

Our prayers ascend like incense to God when we pray in the name of Jesus. For us to effectively pray we must be in him—in union with his life and with his death.

The Holy Spirit is vital to our prayers. His inspiration and guidance in our prayers is crucial because he intercedes for us and actually pleads our case before God (Romans 8:26–27). With his help, our prayers are conformed to the will of God!

Read **Exodus 30:1–10, 34–38**.

What was the altar of incense made of?

_____Acacia wood_____

What precious metal was overlaid on it?

_____Gold_____

What are the dimensions of the altar of incense?

_____1 cubit (1 1/2 ft. or 46 cm) long, 1 cubit (1 1/2 ft. or 46 cm) wide, and 2 cubits (3 ft. or 92 cm) high_____

Where did the altar of incense stand in the Holy Place?

_____In front of the veil_____

What was placed on its four corners?

_____Horns_____

Could the incense also be used as perfume for personal use (see Exodus 30:37–38)?

_____No, it was to be holy to the Lord_____

What Participants Will Learn from This Session

- God is our sustenance for life. Jesus is the "bread from heaven."
- We are in covenant with God.
- Prayer that pleases God is pure and reflective of his will.

Opening the Session (5 minutes)

Summarize last week's lesson:

Last week Pastor Shawn shared with us that the lampstand in the Holy Place was made from one piece of pure gold. The artisans who hammered the lampstand were chosen by God and were filled by the Spirit of God with skill, intelligence, and knowledge to devise artistic designs.

Like the lampstand, you and I have been strategically and purposefully placed in this world to shine Christ for his glory. Jesus said that he is the light of the world and whoever follows him will never walk in darkness, but will have the light of life. God desires to display his light in us that he might be revealed through us.

In this session, we'll look at the other two items in the Holy Place—the table of bread and the altar of incense.

Viewer Guide (30 minutes)

The viewer guide helps participants follow along with Pastor Shawn's teaching as they watch the video.

Session 5
Presence: The Table of Bread and the Altar of Incense

1. Table of Bread (Exodus 25:23–30; Leviticus 24:5–9)

   a. The bread symbolized:

      i. God's __covenant__ with his people (Leviticus 24:8).

      ii. God's __provision__ for his people (Exodus 16:4).

      iii. God's __invitation__ to intimate fellowship at the King's table.

   b. In John 6:22–59, Jesus says that he is "the __bread__ of life."

2. Altar of Incense (Exodus 30:1–10)

   a. The incense symbolized the __prayers__ of the people (Psalm 141:1–2; Revelation 8:3–4; Revelation 5:8; Luke 1:8–13).

   b. Three closing points:

      i. Prayer __ushers__ us into the presence of God.

      ii. God answers the prayers of those who are in right __relationship__ with him.

      iii. Prayer that pleases God is __pure__ and __reflective__ of his will (Matthew 6:7–13; John 14:13–14; James 4:3; 1 John 5:14).

Group Discussion (25 minutes)

Discuss the following questions with your class or small group *after* watching the video.

1. We learned that bread is a symbol of God's provision. When have you seen God provide for you or your family in an unexpected way? What did you learn from that time?

_____

_____

_____

_____

2. The bread of the presence symbolized God's covenant with the people of Israel. Read **Luke 22:14–20**. What covenant does God have with believers today? What is the significance of this covenant?

_____

_____

_____

_____

3. Incense symbolizes prayer and brings us into the presence of God. When have you experienced this truth—a time when you sensed prayer bringing you, or an entire group, into the presence of God?

_____

_____

_____

_____

4. Pastor Shawn said that prayer that pleases God is pure and reflective of God's will. In your own words, what does it mean that our prayer should be pure and reflective?

_____

_____

_____

_____

5. What, if anything, may be hindering answers to your prayers to God right now? Where do you need to trust God more deeply?

_____

_____

_____

_____

Key Scriptures

Old Testament	New Testament
"You gave them bread from heaven for their hunger and brought water for them out of the rock for their thirst." —Nehemiah 9:15	"Truly, truly, I say to you, it was not Moses who gave you the bread from heaven, but my Father gives you the true bread from heaven. For the bread of God is he who comes down from heaven and gives life to the world." —John 6:32–33
"The LORD is far from the wicked, but he hears the prayer of the righteous."—Proverbs 15:29	"And another angel came and stood at the altar with a golden censer, and he was given much incense to offer with the prayers of all the saints on the golden altar before the throne, and the smoke of the incense, with the prayers of the saints, rose before God from the hand of the angel." —Revelation 8:3–4

Group Activity (Optional; 5–10 minutes)

Before your activity time: You'll need a small loaf of crusty bread and some plates and/or napkins (and if you're comfortable with it, wine/juice and cups for everyone—see the "Extra Impact" suggestion below).

At the end of your discussion time, cue your worship music. Bring out the loaf of bread, and ask people to form a circle. Say something like: We've already learned and shared a lot in the past several weeks, and have come increasingly into God's presence together. So before we go any further together, let's use this opportunity to recognize how we've seen God's presence in each other's lives. When the loaf of bread is passed to you, take a piece and pass it to the person on your right. As you pass it along, thank God for the person you're passing it to, and for what he or she has brought to this group. Be as general or specific—or as quiet—as you're comfortable being.

After everyone has had a chance to share and pray, give permission for everyone to eat their piece of bread. As they do, close your activity time in prayer, again thanking God for his presence in each person's life.

Extra Impact: Consider sharing the Lord's Supper (Communion) together in lieu of the above activity—or do both. If possible, you could also consider extending the activity into a potluck meal.

For an activity that focuses on the prayer and the altar of incense, you may want to burn incense and pray the Lord's Prayer together from Matthew 6:9–13.

Our Father in heaven,
hallowed be your name.
Your kingdom come, your will be done,
on earth as it is in heaven.
Give us this day our daily bread,
and forgive us our debts, as we also have forgiven our debtors.
And lead us not into temptation, but deliver us from evil.

What Did the High Priest Do?

God chose the high priest to be the ultimate mediator between God and the Israelites. The high priest needed to be of the priestly tribe of Levi and pure in his lineage as a descendant of Aaron, who was both Moses' brother and the first high priest.

- Being the high priest was not a choice a person could make. It was God who set down the regulations for the office (Hebrews 5:1–5), choosing Aaron and his descendents after him.

- The office was hereditary and generally fell to the oldest son unless some impediment disqualified him. Only the sons of Aaron could become high priests.

- Only the high priest could officiate and conduct certain ceremonies, chiefly the duties assigned for the Day of Atonement. The sacrifices on this day, and most especially the prayers of intercession that took place in the Most Holy Place before the mercy seat, could only be done by the high priest and only on this day in the proper manner.

- The high priest was in charge of the entire priestly order and involved in superintending the other priests and Levites as well (Numbers 3 and 8:14–22).

- The high priest had stricter laws of purity than the people and even regular priests (Leviticus 4:1–12; 21:10–15).

- There was to be only one high priest at any given time, but exceptions did occur, such as during the early monarchy when Zadok and Abiathar shared the office (2 Samuel 20:25).

- Reasons for disqualification could include moral fault, ritual impurity, or physical deformity (Leviticus 21:10–24).

Notes:

Notes:

_____

_____

_____

_____

_____

_____

_____

_____

_____

_____

_____

_____

_____

_____

_____

_____

_____

_____

_____

_____

_____

_____

_____

_____

_____

Separated, Exposed, and Covered:
The Veil, the Ark, and the Mercy Seat

Separated, Exposed, and Covered: The Veil, the Ark, and the Mercy Seat

The Veil

Truth Statement

Our sin separates us from God, but peace with God is available to those who place their faith in Jesus Christ.

Key Verse

"Therefore, since we have been justified by faith, we have peace with God through our Lord Jesus Christ. Through him we have also obtained access by faith into this grace in which we stand, and we rejoice in hope of the glory of God."—Romans 5:1–2

The Ark of the Covenant

Truth Statement

To experience God's presence both now and forever, we must come through his Son, Jesus. There is no other way, no other person.

Key Verse

"Jesus said to him, 'I am the way, and the truth, and the life. No one comes to the Father except through me.'"—John 14:6

The Mercy Seat

Truth Statement

We are covered by God's mercy because Christ has made the just and full payment for our sins.

Key Verse

"[Christ] is the propitiation for our sins, and not for ours only but also for the sins of the whole world."—1 John 2:2

Getting into the Word

This section is designed to familiarize participants (and leaders too) with what they will learn in the video segment. It should be completed by participants sometime during the week *before* the class meeting. (The answers are filled in here.)

The Veil

Read **Exodus 26:31–34.**

What three colors were used in the veil?

1. *Blue*

2. *Purple*

3. *Scarlet (red)*

What was embroidered ("worked into") in the cloth?

Cherubim

What two rooms of the tabernacle did this veil separate?

Holy Place and the Most Holy Place (Holy of Holies)

The Ark of the Covenant

Read **Exodus 25:10–16; Hebrews 9:3–4.**

What was the ark made from?

Acacia wood

What was the ark covered with?

Gold

What three things were placed inside the ark?

1. *Golden jar (urn) of manna*

2. *Aaron's staff*

3. *Tablets of the covenant (Ten Commandments)*

The Mercy Seat

Read **Exodus 25:17–22.**

What two creatures made of gold were placed on the mercy seat? And what direction was their gaze?

Cherubim facing one another and gazing toward the mercy seat

Write out verse 22 and underline "I will meet with you." This phrase is mentioned several times in the book of Exodus. This is the heart of God!

There I will meet with you, and from above the mercy seat, from between the two cherubim that are on the ark of the testimony, I will speak with you about all that I will give you in commandment for the people of Israel.

What Participants Will Learn from This Session

- The veil is a symbol of what would be gained because of Jesus Christ.
- Love and justice collided at the cross, and it's there that God's wrath is satisfied.

Opening the Session (5 minutes)

Summarize last week's lesson:

Last week Pastor Shawn taught on the table of bread and the altar of incense.

The children of Israel were fed by God: "I will rain bread from heaven for you." Because Jesus is the bread of life, he is the provision we need.

As the priests would offer incense on the altar inside the Holy Place, God was pleased with the prayers of his people. He longs for us to pray to him, and he is faithful to answer.

This week we'll pull back the veil and move into the Most Holy Place. We'll learn about the only item that was placed in the holiest of holy places in the presence of God: the ark of the covenant.

Viewer Guide (30 minutes)

The viewer guide helps participants follow along with Pastor Shawn's teaching as they watch the video.

Session 6
Separated, Exposed, and Covered:
The Veil, the Ark, and the Mercy Seat

1. The Veil (Exodus 26:31–33)

    a. The ___blue___ represents God's holiness.

    b. The ___purple___ represents the royalty/kingship of God.

    c. The ___scarlet/red___ represents the sin of humanity (Isaiah 1:18).

    d. Cherubim were ___protectors___ of God's majesty (Genesis 3:24; Revelation 4:6–9).

    e. Our sin ___separates___ us from a holy God (Romans 5:12).

    f. ___Peace___ with God is available to those who place their faith in Jesus Christ (Hebrews 7:26-27; 9:11-12; 1 Peter 3:18; Romans 5:1–2).

2. The Ark of the Covenant (Exodus 37:1–9)

    a. The ark contained (Hebrews 9:4):

        i. The tablets of the _Ten Commandments_ (Exodus 25:16)

        ii. Jar of _manna_ (Exodus 16:31–34)

        iii. Aaron's _staff_ (Numbers 17:10)

    b. The Law (commandments)

        i. Jesus is the _fulfillment_ of the Law (Matthew 5:17).

        ii. The Word/Law was made _flesh_ in Jesus Christ (John 1:14).

        iii. The Law was _revealed_ in and through Jesus (John 14:6).

    c. Jesus is the bread/manna from _heaven_ (John 6:31–33).

    d. Aaron's staff is a symbol of appointment. Jesus is the chosen _Messiah_ (John 1:29–31).

3. The Mercy Seat (Exodus 25:17–22)

    a. The ark exposes our sinfulness; the mercy seat _covers_ us.

    b. _Propitiation_ is a just and full payment for our sins (Leviticus 16:14; 17:11).

    c. _Atonement_ means _"covering"_, that we might be in right relationship with God through Jesus Christ (1 John 2:2).

4. Love and justice collided at the cross, and it's there that God's wrath is _satisfied_.

Group Discussion (25 minutes)

Discuss the following questions with your class or small group *after* watching the video.

1. The veil was the last barrier between God and his people. **Hebrews 10:20** tells us that "the new and living way ... he opened for us through the curtain, that is, through his flesh." Had you previously thought of this Scripture in the literal sense—that Jesus not only tore the curtain, but *was* the curtain? How does this affect your perspective of Jesus, and what he did for us?

    _____

    _____

    _____

    _____

    _____

2. What does it mean to be separated from God? What consequences of this separation do you see in the world today?

    _____

    _____

    _____

    _____

    _____

3. Read **Matthew 5:17–18**. In what ways was Jesus the fulfillment of the Law? What does this truth mean to you, personally?

    _____

    _____

    _____

    _____

    _____

4. Pastor Shawn stated, "Love and justice collided at the cross." When you heard this, what were your thoughts?

_____

_____

_____

_____

_____

5. What is your takeaway from this session? From this study? What do you think God wants you to do in response to it?

_____

_____

_____

_____

_____

Key Scriptures

Old Testament	New Testament
"Come now, let us reason together, says the LORD: though your sins are like scarlet, they shall be as white as snow; though they are red like crimson, they shall become like wool."—Isaiah 1:18	"Where there is forgiveness of these, there is no longer any offering for sin. Therefore brothers, since we have confidence to enter the holy places by the blood of Jesus, by the new and living way that he opened for us through the curtain, that is through his flesh, and since we have a great priest over the house of God. Let us draw near with a true heart in full assurance of faith, with our hearts sprinkled clean from an evil conscience and our bodies washed with pure water." —Hebrews 10:18–22

Group Activity (Optional; 5–10 minutes)

Before your meeting time: Reproduce the following illustration—you can either put this up on a whiteboard and let group members copy it onto their own papers (which you'll provide), or simply provide them with papers with this graphic pre-printed.

After your discussion time, cue your worship music. Say something like, *Over the last six weeks, we've been taken deeper and deeper into the tabernacle, and into God's presence. As we near the end of this study, let's consider how we live out God's presence before others, and how far we allow God to take them into his presence through us.*

Depending on how you've prepared this lesson, either give group members the pre-printed illustration, or give them each a paper and pen and allow them a minute to draw it.

Then, say something like, *Look at the illustration and the different levels—or veils, if you will. At which level in this circle do you no longer feel "safe" living out who you are in Jesus? Mark that place on the circle.*

Allow everyone time to mark their circles. Then discuss the following questions:

- Why did you mark your circle in that place?
- How would believing that God really is present with you everywhere help you to live out your faith more fully? What would that look like for you?

Close your activity time in prayer, asking God to help each of your group members to know and remember who they really are in Jesus, and to give them the strength and courage to live that out even further than they do right now.

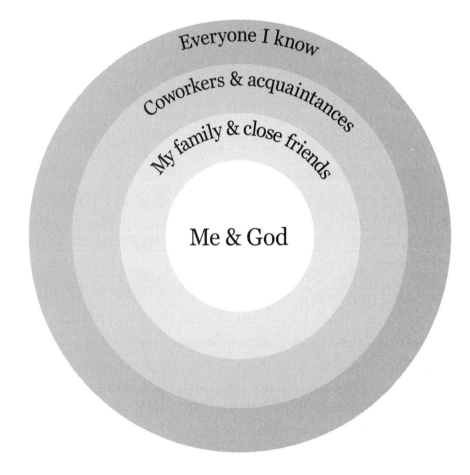

Where Is the Ark Today?

The Old Testament mentions the ark of the covenant for the last time in 2 Chronicles 35:3. There, after finding the book of the law, King Josiah celebrated the Passover. He then instructed the Levites to return the ark to the temple. The New Testament only mentions the ark in John 1:14 (an allusion) and Hebrews 8:2, 5; 9:1-24. Yet, these are references to the Old Testament sacred object.

The ark was likely destroyed in 586 BC when Nebuchadnezzar captured Jerusalem. There is no mention of it in the list of temple treasures that the Babylonian king took (2 Kings 25:13–17). When the exiles later returned to Jerusalem to rebuild the temple, they were allowed to bring several thousand articles from the temple with them. However, there is no mention of the ark (Ezra 1:7–11).

When the Roman general Pompey conquered Jerusalem and entered the Most Holy Place in the temple, he famously affirmed that he had seen nothing but "an empty and mysterious space." Although for Pompey the expression was in reference to images of God, it implies that the ark was absent as well.

Over the centuries there have been claims that the ark survived the Babylonian invasion. In 2 Maccabees 2:4–8 the prophet Jeremiah is said to have hidden the ark in a cave on Mt. Nebo, which is east of the Dead Sea in today's Jordan.

An Ethiopian legend has Menelik, King Solomon's son by the Queen of Sheba, carrying the ark to Ethiopia (a copy of the ark was left behind in Jerusalem). The ark is alleged to be hidden in a church in the city of Axum, where it has been protected by generations of guardian monks.

Jewish tradition says that before the temple was destroyed by the Babylonians, the ark was hidden in a secret underground chamber below the Most Holy Place.

Fueled by the popularity of the movie *Raiders of the Lost Ark*, recent years have seen numerous searches and appeals for money to fund the recovery of the ark. A cave near the Dead Sea or in one of the tunnels under Jerusalem's temple Mount are only two of the suggested locations. Claims of having found the ark have never been accompanied by any pictures or other evidence.

Notes:

_____

_____

_____

_____

_____

_____

_____

_____

_____

_____

_____

_____

_____

_____

_____

_____

_____

_____

_____

_____

_____

_____

_____

_____

SUMMARY

The Courtyard: God's desire is to usher us in from the outer courtyard into the innermost dwelling place of his presence. Just as God brought the Israelites out of Egypt so that they might be brought into a covenant relationship with him, so too God has made a way where we can be free from the bondage of sin and brought into a personal relationship with him through his Son Jesus Christ.

The Altar of Burnt Offering: No longer is the sacrifice of an unblemished animal needed to atone for our sin. Jesus Christ, through his death on the cross, became the sacrifice who would once and for all atone for the sins of all people.

The Laver: Just as the priests had to be cleansed and pure before entering into the Holy Place, we too must be cleansed before we can enter into the presence of God. As the priests would gaze into the laver, they would see their reflection and be reminded of their need to keep their hearts pure. As we gaze into the Word of God, our sinfulness—and our need for repentance—is exposed.

The Lampstand: The lampstand was strategically placed so that it might give light in the Holy Place. In the same way, every person who is truly a follower of Christ has been strategically placed in this world to shine the light of Christ in a dark world so that they may see Christ. For us to shine brightly, we must not let the flame of our witness die out.

The Table of Bread: We have been invited by God to commune with him at his table. Through his Son Jesus Christ, he has invited us into a covenant relationship that is intimate and personal.

The Altar of Incense: God delights in the prayers of his people. As the priests would offer incense on the altar inside the Holy Place, God was pleased with the prayers of his people. He longs for us to pray to him, and he is faithful to answer. The prayers that please God are always those that are pure and reflective of his will.

The Veil: As the priests would enter the Holy Place, they would always see the veil that separated the Holy Place from the Most Holy Place. It was a visual reminder that sin separated man from God. Only once a year could the high priest enter beyond the veil, to the ark and the mercy seat, to make atonement for the sins of the people. However, when Christ died, the veil was torn from top to bottom, symbolizing God's work in bringing us into his presence. Christ's body was torn for us, so that we might enter into the very presence of God.

The Ark and Mercy Seat: The ark was a reminder of the holiness of God and his standard of righteousness. Within the ark was the Law, which exposes the sin of all people. We stand before God guilty. But because of God's grace, there is a mercy seat upon which the blood of the sacrifice was sprinkled—symbolizing the grace of God that covers the sin and guilt for all who put their faith and trust in Jesus Christ.

Christ's Sacrifice

Because of the Father's love for us he gave his son Jesus, the perfect sacrifice, that we may be reconciled to him. Jesus, our Great High Priest, serves in heaven on our behalf.

God's Word further explains that *we also* are now part of his priesthood. First Peter 2:9 reads, "But *you* are a chosen race, a royal priesthood, a holy nation, a people for his own possession, that *you* may proclaim the excellencies of [Christ] who called *you* out of darkness into his marvelous light" (emphasis added).

Through the finished work of our Great High Priest, Jesus, there is no longer one central place of worship where the presence of God can be found. The Old Testament tabernacle is no longer necessary, because God's very presence travels with each and every believer. Just as God's glory and presence invaded the tabernacle of the wilderness, our prayer is that as you surrender to God, his glory will invade your very being, and his Holy Spirit will prompt and guide you from within.

Don't miss this vital life-changing biblical fact: **You are now his tabernacle!**

Scripture declares, "Christ in *you*, the hope of glory!" (Colossians 1:27, emphasis added). Just as the Lord journeyed with the Israelites in the desert, our prayer is that he will travel through life with you.

> "The LORD bless you and keep you; the LORD make His face shine upon you and be gracious to you; the LORD lift up His countenance upon you and give you peace."
> —Numbers 6:24–26 (Aaron's blessing)

Aaron—The brother of Moses. He was from the tribe of Levi and served as high priest in the tabernacle.

Altar of Burnt Offering—The place where the sacrifice was made for the sins of the people.

Ark of the Covenant—The item placed in the Most Holy Place of the tabernacle. It contained the tablets of the law, Aaron's staff, and a jar of manna.

Atonement—Payment for the sins of the people, offered once a year by the high priest. Jesus Christ offered atonement for our sins by shedding his blood on the cross, once and for all.

Courtyard of the Tabernacle—The area in which the priests would make the sacrifice on the altar of burnt offering, as well as cleanse themselves at the laver.

Covenant—An agreement between two parties. God had promised that he would be the God of Israel and they would be his people. In his covenant with Moses, Israel would be blessed if they obeyed him, but if by their choice they refused, God would withhold his blessing.

Day of Atonement/Yom Kippur—The occasion upon which once a year the high priest would enter into the Most Holy Place and make atonement for the sins of the people.

Feast of Tabernacles (Booths)/Sukkot—Held five days after the Day of Atonement, commemorating the journey of the children of Israel and their living in tents or booths (huts) after leaving Egypt on their way to the Promised Land.

High Priest—A representative from the tribe of Levi who would offer atonement once a year for the sins of the people.

Holy—"Set apart"; to be pure before God.

Holy Place—The section of the tabernacle where the priests would tend to the lampstand, the table of the bread of presence, and the altar of incense.

Lampstand—Made of pure gold and placed within the Holy Place to give light within the tabernacle. The priests were responsible for making sure that the oil in the lampstand was full.

Laver—Made of bronze and used by the priests for cleansing, so that they might be set apart and purified.

Law/Torah—Known as the Law of Moses; it was given to Moses by God on Mount Sinai. Also, the first five books of the Bible: Genesis, Exodus, Leviticus, Numbers, and Deuteronomy.

Levites and Priests—The caretakers, guardians, and mediators of the tabernacle.

Mediator—One who goes before another on his or her behalf. Moses was the mediator between God and Israel. Jesus Christ is our mediator before God.

Mercy Seat—The top of the ark of the covenant overshadowed by the wings of the golden cherubim.

Messiah/Christ—God in the flesh, the Son of God, whose name is Jesus. The Messiah became the perfect and unblemished sacrifice, once and for all, for the sins of the world.

Moses—The one whom God chose to deliver the children of Israel from their captivity in Egypt. He was instructed by God to construct the tabernacle.

Most Holy Place (Holy of Holies) —The inner sanctum of the tabernacle, where the high priest would enter once a year to sprinkle the blood of the sacrifice on the mercy seat for the sins of the people.

Propitiation— Just and full payment for our sins, in order to satisfy and turn away God's wrath.

Reconciliation—To bring back what was broken. Sin separates us from God, and it is only through Jesus Christ that we can be reconciled to him.

Sacrifice—The offering of an innocent and unblemished animal to pay for the sins of the people. Jesus Christ, the unblemished Lamb of God, became the ultimate sacrifice for our sins.

Sanctification—To be cleansed and set apart to God and for his purposes.

Sanctuary—"Sacred/holy place"; the place where God's presence would dwell among his people.

Shekinah Glory—The radiance of God's glory that filled the Most Holy Place.

Tabernacle—The portable tent constructed by Moses that would serve as the dwelling place of God's presence in the midst of his people.

Temple—The permanent structure that Solomon first built in Jerusalem, which served as the dwelling place of God's presence among his people Israel.

Twelve Tribes of Israel—Descendants of the twelve sons of Jacob.

BIBLE REFERENCES

Tabernacle in the Wilderness	Reference
Frame	Exodus 26:15–37; 36:20–38
Covering	Exodus 26:7–14; 36:14–19
Second Covering	Exodus 26:14; 35:7, 23; 36:19; 39:34
Curtains	Exodus 26:1–14, 31–37; 29:9–16; 35:15, 17; 36:8–19, 35, 37
Court	Exodus 27:9–17; 38:9–16, 18; 40:8, 33
Holy Place	Exodus 26:31–37; 40:22–26
Most Holy Place	Exodus 2:3–35; 40:20–21
Tabernacle completed	Exodus 39:32
Dedicated and sanctified	Exodus 40; Numbers 7
Preparation for traveling	Numbers 1:51; 4:5–33; 7:6–9
Sanctuary	Exodus 25:8
Tent of Meeting	Exodus 27:21
Tent/Tabernacle	Exodus 33:7
Tent of Testimony	Exodus 38:21; Numbers 1:50; 17:7–8
First tent of meeting	Exodus 33:7–11
Pattern revealed by God to Moses	Exodus 25:9; 26:30; 39:32, 42–43
All strangers and unclean are forbidden to enter	Leviticus 15:31; Numbers 1:51; 19:13, 20
Worship and offerings brought to the tabernacle	Leviticus 17:4; Numbers 10:3; 16:19, 42–43; 20:6; 25:6; 31:54; Deuteronomy 12:5–6, 11–14
Trials conducted at the tabernacle	Deuteronomy 17:8–15
All males to appear before the tabernacle three times a year	Exodus 23:17
Encampment around the tabernacle	Numbers 2
Tabernacle tax	Exodus 30:11–16
Furniture of the tabernacle and its construction	Exodus 25:10–40; 27:1–8, 19; 37; 38:1–8

Tabernacle in the Promised Land	Reference
Tent/Tabernacle	1 Chronicles 5:5
Tent of Testimony	2 Chronicles 24:6
Temple of the Lord	1 Samuel 3:3
Who shall dwell in God's tent?	Psalm 15
At Gilgal	Joshua 4:18–19
At Shiloh	Joshua 18:1, 19:51; Judges 18:31, 20:18, 26–27; 21:19; 1 Samuel 2:14; 4:2, 4; Jeremiah 7:12, 14
At Nob	1 Samuel 21:1–6
At Gibeon	1 Chronicles 21:29
At Zion	1 Chronicles 15:1; 16:1–2; 2 Chronicles 1:4
Brought to the temple by Solomon	2 Chronicles 5:5; 1 Kings 8:1, 4–5

Tabernacle in the New Testament	Reference
Tabernacle alluded to (*eskenosen* means dwelt or pitched his tent)	John 1:14
Priestly functions point to Jesus	Hebrews 8:2, 5; 9:1–24

Other DVD-Based Studies For Individuals or Group Use

Christianity, Cults & Religions
Know what you believe and why!

Christians need to know what they believe. This excellent six-session DVD small group study teaches what the Bible says about God, Jesus, salvation, and more. It compares it to the teachings of other religions and cults. Covers Mormonism, Jehovah's Witnesses, Buddhism, Hinduism, Islam and more. Sessions led by Paul Carden, Director of The Centers for Apologetics Research and former co-host of "Bible Answer Man" radio program.

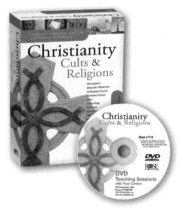

771X Complete Kit *9781596364134*

771DV Leader Pack *9781596364271*

784X Leaders Guide *9781596364288*

785X Participants Guide *9781596364295*

404X Christianity, Cults & Religions pamphlet *9789901981403*

Four Views of the End Times
Cut through the confusion about the *Book of Revelation*

What does the Bible actually say about the end times that lead to the return of Jesus Christ? The differing ideas that divide believers into four major points-of-view are examined in this Four Views of the End Times DVD-based small group study. This new six-session study shows four different Revelation time lines and tackles Dispensational Premillennialism, Postmillennialism, Historic Premillennialism, and Amillennialism. For each view, the objective study includes simple definitions, explanation and discussion of supporting Scriptures, an overview of the view's popularity, and a focus on what we can gain from studying this perspective, and common questions and answers.

770X Complete Kit *9781596364127*

770DV Leader Pack *9781596364240*

782X Leader Guide: Four Views *9781596364257*

783X Participants Guide: Four Views *9781596364264*

350X Four Views of the End Times pamphlet *9781596360891*

Feasts of the Bible
Connect the Hebrew roots of Christianity and the symbolism within each feast

Some Christians miss the importance of the biblical feasts, seeing them as merely "Jewish" holidays, but Scripture says these are the Feasts of the Lord God, established for all people for all time. Now you can connect the Hebrew roots of Christianity and the symbolism within each feast that points to Jesus Christ. The Feasts and Holidays of the Bible will also show you how to conduct your own Christian Passover Seder, where you will learn how all the Old Testament Passover activities point symbolically to Jesus.

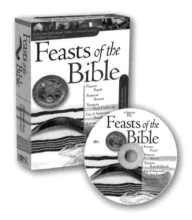

101X Complete Kit *9781596364646*

101DV Leader Pack *9781596364653*

102X Leaders Guide *9781596364660*

103X Participants Guide *9781596364677*

455X Feasts of the Bible pamphlet *9781890947583*

108X Messiah in the Feasts of Israel book *9780970261977*

Christian History Made Easy
People and Events Every Christian Should Know

In this 12-session DVD-based study, Dr. Timothy Paul Jones takes you through the most important events in Christian history from the time of the apostles to today. He brings to life the fascinating people and events that shaped our world. This isn't dry names and dates. It's full of dramatic stories told with a touch of humor. This series, based on Dr. Jones's popular award-winning book Christian History Made Easy, ties in spiritual lessons believers can glean by looking at the past, and shows how God was still working in his church despite all the ups and downs.

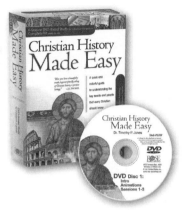

157X Complete Kit 9781596365254

157DV Leader Pack 9781596365261

158X Leaders Guide.. 9781596365278

159X Participants Guide.. 9781596365285

705X Book.. 9781596363281

Other Products from Rose Publishing

Rose Guide to the Temple
The ONLY book on the Temple with clear plastic overlays and 150 color illustrations, diagrams, and charts!

Rose Guide to the Temple is a full-color Christian book that provides a complete easy-to-understand overview of the history of the Temple in Jerusalem. If you enjoy studying God's Word, you will love the fact that Rose Guide to the Temple answers many questions about how the Temple looked during biblical times. Bible scholars and professors will enjoy the well-annotated text. The author is archaeologist and professor Dr. Randall Price, who has spent more than 30 years exploring the Holy Land and studying the Temple.

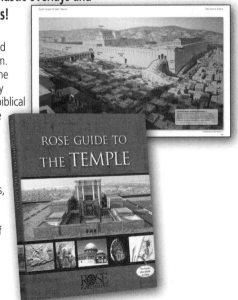

Rose Guide to the Temple has 150 images, charts, diagrams, photos, and illustrations, many of which have never published before, and covers the important events and people in the history of the Temple from Abraham to modern day.

Product Code: **104X**, Hardbound,
ISBN: 9781596364684

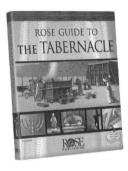

Rose Guide to
The Tabernacle book

Full color, reproducible book on the The Tabernacle, with clear plastic overlays of the coverings of the "tent of meeting." Learn how the sacrifices, utensils, and even the structure of the tabernacle were designed to show us something about God. See the parallels between the Old Testament sacrifices and priests' duties, and Jesus' service as the perfect sacrifice and perfect high priest.

Tabernacle Cutaway

This new Tabernacle Cutaway wall chart provides you with an inside look at the furnishings of the Tabernacle and the high priest's garments. Each part is identified by a number and is explained on a reproducible worksheet on the back of the chart.

Size: 19" x 26". Also available as a 14-panel pamphlet.

PowerPoint® Tabernacle

Microsoft PowerPoint users will love this easy-to-use presentation on the Tabernacle. This fantastic teaching tool allows you to project on a screen—or show or your computer monitor—the text and illustrations of the Tabernacle wall chart.

The Tabernacle Workbook

This 40-page workbook is packed with reproducible activity and information sheets on the Tabernacle, the sacrifices, the furnishings (including the Ark of the Covenant), the priests' garments, and the symbolism that points to Jesus. Make learning fun with worksheets, puzzles, craft ideas, snack ideas, and activities. Perfect for ages 8 to adults.